ISBN 978-0-332-68141-2
PIBN 10987544

This book is a reproduction of an important historical work. Forgotten Books uses
state-of-the-art technology to digitally reconstruct the work, preserving the original format
whilst repairing imperfections present in the aged copy. In rare cases, an imperfection in
the original, such as a blemish or missing page, may be replicated in our edition. We do,
however, repair the vast majority of imperfections successfully; any imperfections that
remain are intentionally left to preserve the state of such historical works.

REPORT

OF THE

𝕮reasurer and 𝕽eceiber-𝕲eneral

OF THE

COMMONWEALTH OF MASSACHUSETTS,

FOR THE YEAR ENDING

DECEMBER 31, 1869.

BOSTON:

WRIGHT & POTTER, STATE PRINTERS,

79 MILK STREET, (CORNER OF FEDERAL.)

1870.

ot
our
f this
al banks

Commonwealth of Massachusetts.

TREASURY DEPARTMENT, BOSTON, }
January 25, 1870.. }

on. HARVEY JEWELL, *Speaker of the House of Representatives.*

SIR :—I have the honor to transmit through you to the legis-
ture my Annual Report as Treasurer and Receiver-General of
e Commonwealth for the year ending December 31, 1869.

I am, with respect,
    Your obedient servant,

JACOB H. LOUD,
Treasurer and Receiver-General.

.ot
; our
.f this
al banks

Commonwealth of Massachusetts.

TREASURY DEPARTMENT, BOSTON,
January 25, 1870.

To the Honorable Senate and House of Representatives.

The undersigned, in obedience to the requirements of law, transmits herewith his Annual Report of the operations of the Treasury Department for the fiscal year ending December 31, 1869.

The financial condition of the State is always a subject of especial interest to the people. Never has there been a more pressing need of care and prudence in the application and disposal of the public revenues and in the preservation of the credit of the State, than at the present time. The debt of the Commonwealth is already large and must necessarily increase during the next four years, until the completion of the public works now in progress. Our State credit, both at home and abroad, ranks higher than that of any other State in the Union. It would be unwise to weaken the confidence everywhere expressed both in our ability and our disposition to meet our obligations, by embarking in any new enterprises. While our debt has largely increased, it is gratifying to note also the material increase in the valuation of property in the Commonwealth liable to taxation, during the last year.

The following is a comparison of the last two years, as compiled from the returns of the assessors of the several cities and the report of the Savings Bank Commissioner and the ... made to the Tax Department.

	1868.	1869.
Assessors' aggregate of real and personal property, ...	$1,220,305,939 00	$1,341,169,403 00
Savings Bank deposits, .	94,838,336 00	112,119,016 00
Corporate excess over real estate and machinery, ...	92,326,758 00	95,167,745 00
	$1,407,471,033 00	$1,548,456,164 00
		1,407,471,033 00
Increase in 1869 in taxable values, . .		$140,985,131 00

The addition of half a million dollars to the State tax and the reduction of expenditures during the last year has produced a very considerable improvement in the financial results of the year, as compared with the previous year.

ABSTRACT OF RECEIPTS AND PAYMENTS.
Receipts.

Total receipts in revenue for the year 1869, .	$5,722,394 91
Total receipts and credits on account of the sinking funds, loans and other accounts for 1869, ...	11,329,353 84
Cash on hand January 1, 1869, . . .	1,161,932 80
	$18,213,681 55

Payments.

Total payments on account of ordinary expenses for the year 1869, ...	$5,450,227 47
Total payments on account of the several sinking funds, loans and other accounts, . .	10,620,645 27
Cash on hand January 1, 1870, . . .	2,142,808 81
	$18,213,681 55

The receipts in revenue in 1869 exceed those of the previous year in the sum of $612,458.68 and they also exceed the amounts charged to ordinary expenses by $272,167.44 against a deficiency of $798,742.25 at the close of 1868.

The amount charged to expenses in 1869 is less than the amount charged in the previous year by $458,451.01.

In the payments charged to ordinary expenses is included the sum of $195,250 paid into the bounty loan and war loan sinking funds as required by the Acts establishing said funds. These contributions to the sinking funds will not be required hereafter, as these funds have reached a sum which with the accumulations of interest will be sufficient to pay the scrip at maturity. There is also included the payment of grants made to educational and charitable institutions and other objects not likely to be renewed. With the exception of the interest on the public debt, which must necessarily increase until the Hoosac Tunnel is completed, it is confidently expected that a still further reduction in the expenditures of the government may be made without detriment.

REVENUE.

The principal sources of revenue are the tax on savings bank deposits, the corporation tax, taxes on non-resident stockholders in national banks, insurance premiums, coal and mining companies and receipts from alien passengers, correctional institutions, licenses and commissions and interest on deposits. It may safely be assumed that the income from these sources for the coming year will be equal to that of the last, and from some of them the receipts will be considerably increased. The savings bank tax alone yielded more than $200,000 over that of the preceding year. Unless new objects of taxation can be availed of, the deficiency of these to meet the annual expenditures must be raised by a tax upon the polls, property and estates in the Commonwealth.

CORPORATION TAX.

The corporation tax law has been a source of considerable revenue during the year.

There has been collected,	$1,158,989 70
There has been distributed,	1,050,720 05
Leaving a balance in the Treasury of	$408,269 65

this amount a portion will be paid over to cities and towns the provisions of the Act, while a considerable amount is still due from corporations, so that the actual revenue derived from the operation of the law will be about the same as last year.

The general principles of the law have now been passed upon by the supreme court, both of the State and the United States, and the law may confidently be considered as a source of constant and considerable revenue.

TAX ON NATIONAL BANK SHARES.

By the provisions of chapter 345 of the Acts of the year 1868, a considerable modification was made in the system of taxing the shares of non-resident holders in national banks. The first congressional act, June 30, 1864, creating national banks, provided for taxing their shares, in the place where the bank was located, to the owners thereof. By chapter 242 of the Acts of the legislature of the year 1865, provisions were made for taxing our citizens in the towns or cities where they resided, for all the shares which they held in national banks. The supreme court of the Commonwealth decided in some cases brought before them that under this Act taken in connection with the National Banking Act, our citizens were so taxable for shares in banks located in this State, but not for shares in banks located out of the State.

Austin *vs.* Aldermen of Boston, 14 Allen, 359.
Flint *vs.* Aldermen of Boston, 99 Mass. 141.

This construction of the law was substantially adopted by Congress by the Amendatory Act of February 10, 1868.

The plan of taxation introduced by the National Banking Act, removes altogether from the burden of our local taxation shares in banks located out of the State and subjects them to the burdens of another State, contrary to what has been generally if not universally recognized as a fundamental principle in taxation, that personal property shall bear the burden of taxation in the domicil of its owner. As an exchange, however, the right is conferred upon the State where the banks are located, of imposing a tax upon the shares of non-residents. It would seem that the congressional Act might be readily so modified as either not to interfere with the old and well established plan of taxing o citizens for their personal property where they reside, or if is is for reasons of public policy impossible, that the national banks

might be made subject to the plan of taxation adopted by the State
for corporations chartered by its authority. By provisions of
chapter 345, Acts of 1868, the assessors of the several cities and
towns are in substance required to assess on and the collectors
to collect from non-resident shareholders in national banks
located in their respective cities or towns, a tax of the same
proportionate amount as is assessed upon and collected from
the residents of that town on account of owning the same or
other kinds of personal property. Returns of assessment are to
be made upon the completion of the assessment and the amounts
received to be paid over and accounted for to the Treasurer of
the Commonwealth, on or before the first Monday of December
in each year. This Act was passed late in the session of 1868,
but although assessments were generally made in that year, the
collectors in many cases failed to collect the taxes which were
assessed, as much resistance was offered to the payment under
a real or alleged belief of the unconstitutionality of the act.
Cases, however, arose in Boston, which were fully and thoroughly
argued before the supreme court during the last year, which
involved all the questions relating to the general frame and
purpose of the Act, and the decisions of the court fully sustained
its constitutionality.

Providence Institution of Savings *vs.* the City of Boston.
Pliny Jewell *vs.* the City of Boston.
Providence Institution of Savings *vs.* F. U. Tracy.
Pliny Jewell *vs.* F. U. Tracy.

The taxes for the year 1869 have been mostly assessed and
collected with a good degree of promptness and completeness.
There are, however, some towns from which a part only of the
returns required have been received.

From the returns received it appears that the whole
amount assessed for 1868 and 1869 was, . . $312,194 11
Expenses of assessing and collecting, etc., reported, 2,089 75
Not collected or retained for expenses of assessing
and collecting, ... 82,068 55

Net result to Dec. 31, 1869, ... $228,035 81

his amount is an addition to the revenues of the State, and
·htening the amount necessary to be raised by direct taxa-

tion for the purposes of the State, relieves each city and town in proportion to their share of a State tax of the same amount.

In the present condition of national legislation upon this subject, I consider it very improbable that any beneficial change can be made in the general frame and purpose of the law. In several important matters relating to the execution of the law, I would recommend further legislation; especially for the purposes of securing a prompt and efficient compliance with its present requirements and of fixing a uniform scale of allowances for assessments and collections.

THE PUBLIC DEBT.

The debt of the Commonwealth, which includes not only the civil and war debt, but also the entire amount of State scrip issued on account of the Troy and Greenfield Railroad and Hoosac Tunnel, and in aid of other railroad enterprises, now outstanding, amounted at the close of the financial year Dec. 31, 1869, to, ... $30,823,380 02

This is an increase of the debt in 1869 of, . 3,087,509 97

Being an increase of the funded debt of, . . 2,589,840 00

And of the unfunded or temporary debt of, . 497,669 97

The funded debt was increased by the issue of scrip under the provisions of chapter 450 of the Acts of 1869, to the Boston, Hartford and Erie Railroad Company during the

year, ... $3,102,440 00

And decreased by payments on account of scrip loaned Western
Railroad, ... $435,600 00
Scrip loaned Eastern Railroad, . 75,000 00
Scrip to fund the public debt, . 2,000 00
———————— 512,600 00
——————————

Making the net increase as above, . $2,589,840 00

The increase of the temporary debt from last year is represented by certificates of conditional indebtedness issued to Walter Shanly and Francis Shanly, for work done by them under their contract to construct the Hoosac Tunnel, and by payments made for interest on the scrip heretofore issued for the prosecution of that work and for other expenditures on the same account, for which money has not been raised by a sale of scrip as contemplated by law.

The funded debt is now, ...	$29,397,260 00
The temporary debt is now, ...	1,426,120 02
	$30,823,380 02

It has thus been made to appear that the entire addition to the debt during the year was caused by the loan of the State credit in aid of certain railroad enterprises, which otherwise would have failed of completion, for the still further development of the commercial and industrial interests of the State, and that no portion thereof has been occasioned by any failure of the revenue to meet the ordinary expenses of the government, including the liberal grants and appropriations made for educational, charitable and reformatory objects and for the interest on the public debt. While the debt has increased, the means for its final liquidation and payment have also increased, and in a much greater proportion. The present value of the sinking funds is nearly twelve million dollars against thirty million dollars of liabilities, a large part of which will not become due until the expiration of twenty years, and a considerable portion not until thirty years from the present time. More than four million dollars of the scrip included in the debt is held in the funds and is equivalent to a payment of the debt to that extent.

The magnitude of the debt, however, is sufficient to demand the most rigid economy in our expenditures, when we reflect that the annual interest on the debt chargeable upon the revenue already exceeds a million of dollars, and that any considerable increase must of necessity add to the annual State tax.

THE SINKING FUNDS AND THEIR APPLICATION TO THE DEBT.

In showing the relation of the sinking funds to specific portions of the debt, it will afford greater clearness to the statement to divide the debt into two classes. First, the State debt proper, as follows :—

State Almshouse Loan, ...	$210,000 00
Enlargement of State House, ...	165,000 00
Lunatic Hospital, Taunton, ...	94,000 00
Lunatic Hospital, Northampton, . . .	50,000 00
Consolidation of Statutes,*	150,000 00
Funding the Public Debt, ...	200,000 00
Back Bay Lands, ...	220,000 00
War Debt, ...	16,573,244 00
Overdue scrip 1856, not presented, . . .	1,000 00
	$17,663,244 00

There are seven distinct sinking funds created for the payment of this portion of the debt, and the amount of each December 31, 1869, was as follows :—

Almshouse Loan Sinking Fund, . . .	$147,758 47
Debt Extinguishment Sinking Fund, . . .	605,400 00
Back Bay Lands, " " . . .	220,000 00
Union Loan, ...	3,600,000 00
Bounty Loan	2,093,837 62
War Loan . " . .	1,175,907 30
Coast Defence Loan " " . .	398,936 34
	$8,241,839 73

In this class is included $350,000† not chargeable upon these funds, to become due within two years and to be paid out of the revenue.

To the above there might be added the balance standing to the credit of the Commissioners on Public Lands of $236,922.68, growing out of the unexpended moiety of sales of the Back Bay Lands. Most of the unsold lands in the Back Bay are filled, and the moiety of the future sales will doubtless be adequate to any payments necessary to the development of this enterprise. So that a large part of the present balance to their account might be carried to the War Loan Sinking Fund, as contemplated by law, but it will need additional legislation to effect the transfer.

* Paid January 1, 1870.
† $150,000 of this debt was paid Jan. 1, 1870, out of revenue.

It is safe to assume that the present amount of these funds, with the accumulations of interest thereon, will be sufficient to pay at maturity this portion of the debt.

Second. The railroad debt, which includes the amount of State scrip issued in aid of the several railroad enterprises and is the balance of the funded debt not in the first class. The amount of each outstanding December 31, 1869, is as follows :—

Western Railroad Debt, ...	$3,143,096 00
Eastern " "	125,000 00
Norwich and Worcester Railroad Debt, . .	400,000 00
Troy and Greenfield Railroad and Hoosac Tunnel Debt, ...	4,673,080 00
Boston, Hartford and Erie Railroad Debt, .	3,392,840 00
	$11,734,016 00

The sinking funds applicable to this portion of the debt Dec. 31, 1869, were as follows :—

Western Railroad Sinking Fund, . . .	$1,521,642 10
Norwich and Worcester R. R. Sinking Fund, .	262,025 00
Troy and Greenfield R. R. " " .	619,614 50
Boston, Hartford and Erie R. R. " " .	560,686 00
	$2,963,967 60

This portion of the debt originated in the loan of the credit of the State to the several corporations above named. The State cannot possibly lose anything on account of the first three named. Although the Western Railroad Sinking Fund, in consequence of the amount heretofore paid for exchange, very materially augmented by the high price of gold to redeem the scrip as it matured, will not of itself be sufficient to extinguish the debt, the Boston and Albany Railroad Company is abundantly able to save the State harmless.

The Eastern Railroad debt is paid by money furnished by the Eastern Railroad Company, and there will be no other loss to the State, except the premium paid for gold, while it receives nly currency from the company.

The Norwich and Worcester Railroad Sinking Fund will be ample to redeem the scrip as it becomes due.

The Boston, Hartford and Erie debt, above mentioned, is the amount of sterling scrip issued to that company to December 31, 1869, £701,000, which reduced to Federal money at $4.84, is $3,392,840.00. By the provisions of the Act authorizing the issue of this scrip, that company is required to pay to the commissioners of the sinking fund within thirty days after the delivery of the scrip such a sum as the governor and council shall direct, not less than shall with the accumulations produce at the maturity of such scrip an amount equal to the scrip so issued. The amount of the fund so furnished, with interest, to Dec. 31, 1869, was $560,686. The company has also deposited in the State Treasury " Berdell Mortgage Bonds" to the amount of $3,600,000. This plan of operations would seem to secure the State against any other liability than a failure on the part of that company to pay the interest on the State scrip.

The security of the Commonwealth for the excess of the Troy and Greenfield Railroad and Hoosac Tunnel debt over the amount which shall at its maturity be in the sinking fund, is alone in the value of the property itself.

The following statement exhibits the public debt in detail, the purpose for which the scrip was issued, the times when it will become due and the rate of interest each portion bears and when payable.

FUNDED PUBLIC DEBT JANUARY 1, 1870.

LOANS TO RAILROAD CORPORATIONS.

WESTERN RAILROAD CO.

Interest at 5 per cent., payable in London.

Amount due Apr. 1, 1870, .	.	£180,000
due Apr. 1, 1871, .	.	157,400
due July 1, 1888, .	.	312,000
		£649,400
At $4.84 per £ is		. $3,143,096 00

TROY AND GREENFIELD RAILROAD AND HOOSAC TUNNEL.

Interest at 5 per cent., payable in London.

Amount due Oct. 1, 1888, .	.	£22,500
due Oct. 1, 1889, .	.	29,300
Carried forward, .	.	£51,800

Brought forward, . .	£51,800	$3,143,096 00
Amount due Oct. 1, 1890, . .	62,700	
due Apr. 1, 1888, . .	610,000	
	£724,500	
At $4.84 per £ is . .	$3,506,580 00	

Dollar Bonds, Interest at 5 per cent.,
    payable at Treasury.

Amount due Apr. 1, 1891, . .	216,500 00	
due Apr. 1, 1893, . .	200,000 00	
due Oct. 1, 1893, . .	550,000 00	
		4,473,080 00

SOUTHERN VERMONT RAILROAD CO.

Interest at 5 per cent., payable at Treasury.

Amount due Apr. 1, 1890, ...	200,000 00

EASTERN RAILROAD CO.

Interest at 5 per cent., payable at Treasury.

Amount due July 1, 1870, . .	$75,000 00	
due July 1, 1871, . .	50,000 00	
		125,000 00

NORWICH AND WORCESTER RAILROAD CO.

Interest at 6 per cent., payable at Treasury.

Amount due July 1, 1877, ...	400,000 00

BOSTON, HARTFORD AND ERIE RAILROAD CO.

Interest at 5 per cent., payable in London.

Amount due Jan. 1, 1900, . .	£701,000	
At $4.84 per £ is	3,392,840 00	
Total of Loans to Railroad Corporations, .		$11,734,016 00

FOR ACCOUNT OF PUBLIC INSTITUTIONS, &c.
STATE ALMSHOUSES.

Interest at 5 per cent., payable at Treasury.

Amount due Nov. 1, 1872, .	$100,000 00	
due Oct. 1, 1873, .	60,000 00	
due Oct. 2, 1874, .	50,000 00	
		$210,000 00

STATE HOUSE.

Amount due Oct. 1, 1873, .	$65,000 00	
due Oct. 2, 1874, .	100,000 00	
		165,000 00

LUNATIC HOSPITAL AND STATE PRISON,

Amount due July 1, 1874, ...	94,000 00
Carried forward, ...	$469,000 00

Brought forward, ...	$469,000 00	$11,734,016 00

HOSPITAL IN WESTERN MASSACHUSETTS.
Interest at 6 per cent., payable at Treasury.

Amount due June 1, 1877, ...	50,000 00	

REVISION OF GENERAL STATUTES.
Interest at 5 per cent., payable at Treasury.

Amount due January 1, 1870, ...	150,000 00	

FUNDING PUBLIC DEBT, 1861.
Payable at Treasury.

Amount due June 1, 1870, 5 per ct.,	$21,000 00	
due June 1, 1872, 5 per ct.,	17,000 00	
due June 1, 1870, 6 per ct.,	79,000 00	
due June 1, 1872, 6 per ct.,	83,000 00	
due June 1, 1862, 6 per ct.,		
(not called for,) . .	1,000 00	
		201,000 00

FILLING BACK BAY.
Interest at 5 per cent., payable at Treasury.

Amount due May 1, 1880, ...	220,000 00	
Total for account of Public Institutions, &c.,		1,090,000 00

WAR EXPENDITURES.
UNION FUND LOAN.

Amount due July 1, 1871, 6 per ct.,	$200,000 00	
due July 1, 1872, 6 per ct.,	350,000 00	
due July 1, 1873, 6 per ct.,	300,000 00	
due July 1, 1874, 6 per ct.,	300,000 00	
due July 1, 1875, 6 per ct.,	420,000 00	
due July 1, 1876, 6 per ct.,	1,430,000 00	
due July 1, 1877, 5 per ct.,	400,000 00	
due July 1, 1878, 5 per ct.,	200,000 00	
	$3,600,000 00	

COAST DEFENCES.

Amount due July 1, 1883, 5 per ct., . . .	888,000 00	

BOUNTY LOAN.
Interest at 5 per cent.

Amount due July 1, 1893, .	$200,000 00	
due May 1, 1894, .	4,379,500 00	
due May 1, 1894, £826,-		
600 at $4.84, is, . . .	4,000,744 00	
	8,580,244 00	

Carried forward, ...	$13,068,244 00	$12,824,016 00

Brought forward, ... $13,068,244 00 $12,824,016 00

WAR LOAN.
Currency 5-20.

Amount due Sept. 1, 1886, 6 per ct., . .	3,505,000 00	
Total War Expenditures, . . .	————	16,573,244 00

TEMPORARY DEBT.

Certificates of conditional indebtedness issued to		
W. & F. Shanly, ...	$340,000 00	
Balance of account due Baring Bros. & Co., .	356,989 77	
Deposit loan overdue and unpaid, . . .	3,000 00	
Temporary loan of 1869, ...	722,930 25	
Three years loan overdue and unpaid, . .	3,200 00	
Total temporary debt, . . .	————	1,426,120 02

$30,823,380 02

INTEREST AND PREMIUM ON GOLD.

The amount charged to ordinary revenue in 1869 for interest on the public debt, gold and currency, is .   . $1,074,761 24

Of this sum there was paid at the		
Treasury in gold, . . .	$539,022 50	
and in currency, ...	301,562 99	
Bounty Loan interest on sterling bonds in London, cost in currency, ...	234,175 75	
	—————	$1,074,761 24

There has also been paid and charged to the Troy and Greenfield Railroad and Hoosac Tunnel gold interest on dollar bonds, payable at the Treasury,   .   . $57,787 50 and on sterling bonds in London, cost in currency, 203,388 61

$261,176 11

The amount paid for premium on gold is .   . $170,561 37

This includes the payment of $75,000, for bonds due in 1869 by the Eastern Railroad, together with interest $10,000; and interest on account of Norwich and Worcester Railroad, $24,000; all these sums being paid by the roads in currency.

TRUST FUNDS OF THE COMMONWEALTH.

These are seven in number. The amount of each, Dec. 31, 1869, is as follows:—

Massachusetts School Fund, ...	$2,203,403 77
Fund for the promotion of Education in Agriculture and the Mechanic Arts,. . . .	206,529 00
Todd Normal School Fund, ...	12,100 00
School Fund for Indians, ...	2,500 00
Rogers Book Fund, ...	1,000 00
Charles River and Warren Bridges Fund, . .	65,884 71
Essex Bridge Fund, ...	6,140 81
	$2,497,558 29

Five of these funds are for educational purposes, and there is no provision for the enlargement of any of them except the Massachusetts School Fund, and that has increased during the year $14,512.85.

The Bridges Funds will soon disappear from the list, and the balance of those funds unexpended will be distributed to the cities and towns by whom their maintenance will hereafter be sustained. A list of the securities in which these funds are invested is appended to this Report.

INDIAN SCHOOL FUNDS.

By the provisions of chapter 36 of the General Statutes, certain portions of the income of the Massachusetts School Fund, and of the Indian School Fund, are to be paid to the Guardian of the Christiantown and Chappequiddic Indians, to be applied to the support of public schools among them.

The enfranchisement of the Indians of the Commonwealth, by chapter 463 of the Acts of 1869, seems practically to have annulled the guardianship, and there is now no one authorized to receive and expend said moneys. There is at present an unpaid warrant in the Treasury for seventy-two dollars, without any agent authorized to receive and expend the same. The change in the relation of the Indians to the Commonwealth seems to render some legislation necessary in regard to these funds.

BOUNTIES PAID TO MASSACHUSETTS VOLUNTEERS.

Amount paid to Jan. 1, 1869, was $9,899,732 62

    . paid in 1869,   .   .   1,225 00

                                $9,900,957 62

MONTHLY BOUNTIES.

Amount paid to Jan. 1, 1869,   . $3,078,775 35

         paid in 1869,   .   .   1,974 40

                                3,080,749 75

INTEREST PAID TO MASSACHUSETTS VOLUNTEERS.

Amount paid to Jan. 1, 1869,   . $27,664 72

         paid in 1869,   .   ..   573 69

                                28,238 41

STATE AID TO SOLDIERS AND THEIR FAMILIES.

Amount paid to Jan. 1, 1869, $10,239,182 29

         paid in 1869 to cities

          and towns,   .   .   648,380 60

         paid to non - resident

          widows and children,   7,318 67

                            10,894,881 56

Re-imbursement to cities and towns of bounties

   paid, ...   3,418,640 50

Total payments to soldiers and their families to

   Jan. 1, 1870, ... $27,323,467 84

All which is respectfully submitted.

                           JACOB H. LOUD,

                  Treasurer and Receiver-General.

RECEIPTS, PAYMENTS, AND STATEMENTS IN DETAIL.

RECEIPTS OF. REVENUE.

State Tax, 1868, ...	$12,880 00
State Tax, 1869, ...	2,483,636 46
Non-residents Bank Tax, . . .	197,489 10
Savings Bank Tax, ...	771,998 10
Corporation Tax, ...	1,446,893 27
Annual Insurance Tax, ...	86,269 41
Semi-annual Insurance Tax, . . .	62,506 53
Coal and Mining Companies Tax, . . .	12,081 26
Tax on Hospital Life Insurance Company, .	112,061 61
on Life Insurance Companies, . . .	15,757 43
Alien Estates, ·	1,677 72
Railroad Companies, ...	1,280 00
Alien Passengers, ...	52,535 33
Courts of Insolvency, fees, . . .	2,411 00
Tax on Sales of Liquor, ...	37,775 05
Liquor Licenses, ...	2,675 00
Secretary's Fees, ...	480 63
Commissions issued, ...	6,080 00
Peddlers' Licenses, ...	14,104 00
Insurance Licenses, ...	16,850 00
Receipts at State Reform School, . .	18,542 00
at Tewksbury Almshouse, . .	3,399 32
at Monson " . .	176 57
at Bridgewater, " . .	5,700 08
at Rainsford Island Hospital, . .	508 11
Board of State Charities, . . .	12,353 11
Bastardy and Settlement Cases, . .	7,604 25
Receipts at Nautical Br. State Reform School,	6,668 74
at Industrial School for Girls, . .	2,238 84
State Prison, Labor of Convicts, . .	132,466 74
Premium on Exchange, ...	56,088 36
Income Union Loan Sinking Fund, . .	96,555 00
Back Bay Lands Fund, . .	1,994 04
Interest on Semi-annual Insurance Tax, .	49
on Annual Insurance Tax, . .	27 87
on Coal and Mining Companies, .	15 17
on Deposits, ...	27,230 04
Carried forward, ...	$5,709,010 63

Brought forward, ...	$5,709,010 63	
Interest on Corporation Tax, ...	540 26	
Council Contingent, ...	537 20	
Executive Contingent, ...	866 66	
Surveyor-General of Lumber, ...	316 53	
Attorney-General's fees, costs, &c., . . .	178 58	
State Police, ...	849 91	
Expenses Supreme Judicial Court, . . .	423 80	
Electoral College, ...	6 00	
Rent Back Bay Lands, ...	500 00	
Theodore Lyman, returned, ...	200 00	
Percentage on State Tax, ...	249 36	
Gas Light Companies, ...	3,914 13	
Sale of W. S. Thacher, ...	915 00	
Monthly Bounties, ...	403 99	
Quartermaster-General and Ordnance Department, ...	1,793 83	
Quartermaster supplies, ...	628 65	
Paymasters' Monthly Bounties, . . .	337 32	
Militia Bounty, ...	18 00	
Interest on Temporary Loans, ...	705 06	
		$5,722,394 91

RECEIPTS ON ACCOUNT OF LOANS, SINKING FUNDS AND OTHER ACCOUNTS.

Norwich and Worcester Railroad Sinking Fund,	$10,000 00
Bonds and Mortgages Railroad Companies, .	510,600 00
Western Railroad Sinking Fund, . .	329,927 30
Boston, Hartford and Erie Railroad Loan, .	3,102,440 00
Sales of Back Bay Lands, . . .	458,767 67
Commissioners on Public Lands, . .	229,383 83
Notes and Mortgages Back Bay Lands, . .	373,804 76
Interest on Notes and Mortgages Back Bay Lands, ...	20,465 19
Income Massachusetts School Fund, 1869, .	156,657 94
Todd Normal School Fund, . . .	726 00
School Fund for Indians, . . .	171 50
Rogers Book Fund, ...	60 00
Temporary Loans, ...	1,837,033 20
Conditional Loan to W. & F. Shanly, .	340,000 00
Baring Brothers & Co., ...	464,091 39
Transactions with the Funds, . . .	2,838,915 28
South Boston Flats, ...	545,505 00
Harbor Compensation Fund, . . .	2,210 98
Income Agricultural Fund, . . .	15,605 28
Carried forward, ...	$11,236,365 32

Brought forward, ...	$11,236,365 32	$5,722,394 91
Norwich and Worcester Railroad Interest, .	24,000 00	
Eastern Railroad Interest, ...	10,000 00	
Interest on Troy and Greenfield R. R. Loan; .	37,300 00	
Income Back Bay Lands Sinking Fund, . .	6,600 67	
Hoosac Tunnel and Troy and Greenfield Railroad, ...	13,577 87	.
Massachusetts Volunteers, ...	160 52	
Recruitment Fund, ...	1,349 46	
		11,329,353 84
Cash on hand January 1, 1869, ...		1,161,932 80
Total, ...		$18,213,681 55

PAYMENTS.

Executive Department.

Governor,	$5,000 00	
Governor's Private Secretary,	2,000 00	
Lieutenant-Governor and Council,	17,995 00	
Messengers to Governor and Council,	800 00	
Council Contingent,	1,731 60	
Military Contingent,	2,000 00	
Council Postage and Printing,	621 63	
Executive Contingent,	8,077 65	
		$38,225 88
Secretary's Department.		
Secretary and two Clerks,	$6,200 00	
Secretary's extra Clerks,	15,867 08	
Messenger,	1,183 34	
Incidentals,	4,726 15	
		27,976 57
Treasurer's Department.		
Treasurer and three Clerks,	$9,375 00	
extra Clerks,	2,600 00	
Incidentals,	291 86	
		12,266 86
Tax Commissioner's Bureau,		15,687 80
Auditor's Department.		
Auditor and two Clerks,	$6,400 00	
extra Clerks,	5,319 72	
Incidentals,	454 00	
		12,173 72
Legislative.		
Senate Compensation,	$34,960 00	
Mileage,	347 00	
Blanks and Circulars,	900 00	
Stationery,	1,078 00	
House Compensation,	205,630 00	
Mileage,	2,070 00	
Circulars, &c.,	1,000 00	
Stationery,	2,467 90	
Carried forward,	$248,452 90	$106,330 83

Brought forward, ...	$248,452 90		$106;330 83
Chaplains Senate and House, ...	800 00		
Preacher of Election Sermon, ...	100 00		
Electoral College, ...	191 00		
Sergeant-at-Arms, ...	2,500 00		
Printing, Stationery, &c., ordered by Sergeant-			
at-Arms, ...	1,240 23		
Legislative Contingent, ...	4,525 46		
Clerks Senate and House, ...	7,200 00		
Doorkeepers, Messengers and Pages, . . .	19,355 50		
Witness fees before Committees, . . .	269 96		
Expenses of Committees, ...	6,453 16		
Printing and Binding for Senate and House, .	25,036 95		
			316,125 16
Insurance Commissioner, Clerks, &c., . . .			17,003 03
Commissioner on Savings Banks, ...			3,000 00

State House.

Safe for Treasurer's office, ...	$8,650 00		
Engineers, Watchmen and Firemen, . .	8,942 67		
Fuel and Light, ...	2,667 18		
Repairs, Improvements and Furniture, .	16,325 96		
Commissioners on State House, . .	9,812 40		
			46,398 21

Printing.

Gould's Invertebratæ, ...	$2,153 81		
Term Reports, ...	4,567 50		
Publishing Bank Returns, ...	40 75		
Provincial Laws, ...	5,309 79		
Printing Blue Book, ...	6,132 70		
General Laws, ...	6,000 00		
Supplement, . .	500 00		
Publishing Laws, ...	400 00		
Printing Shareholders in National Bank, . .	5,004 44		
Public Documents, ...	31,729 20		
Special Laws, ...	5,745 56		
Assessors' Books, ...	1,851 10		
Records of Massachusetts Soldiers, .	25,005 71		
			94,440 56

Judiciary.

Judges Supreme Judicial Court, . . .	$29,875 01		
Clerk " " " . . .	3,000 00		
Expenses " " " . . .	1,343 73		
Judges Superior Court, ...	42,751 70		
Probate and Insolvency, . .	21,325 00		
Registers " " . . .	19,450 00		
Carried forward, ...	$117,745 44		$583,297 79

Brought forward, ...	$117,745 44	$583,297 79
Assistant Registers, ...	6,800 00	
Reporter of Decisions, ...	300 00	
Expenses of Courts of Insolvency, . .	258 46	
Justices Police and Municipal Courts, . .	42,108 84	
Clerks " " " . .	13,666 65	
Clerk for Attorney of Suffolk County, . .	458 51	
District-Attorneys, ...	15,187 90	
Attorney-General and Assistant, . . .	5,300 00	
Law Library, . . .	233 60	
Incidentals, ...	1,242 73	
		203,301 63

Agricultural Department.

Secretary Board of Agriculture, . . .	$3,814 09	
Expenses, .	287 32	
Travel Members of Board, ...	1,493 03	
Incidentals of Board, ...	94 58	
Lectures on Agriculture, ...	150 00	
Agricultural Societies, ...	16,933 87	
Cattle Commissioners, ...	2,196 00	
Pleuro-Pneumonia, ...	31 25	
Printing Report of Secretary, ...	10,000 00	
		35,000 14

Charitable.

Expenses Tewksbury Almshouse, . . .	$77,618 72	
Monson Almshouse, ...	52,616 20	
Bridgewater Almshouse, . . .	31,794 97	
Rainsford Island Hospital, . . .	1,981 87	
Asylum for Blind, ...	28,750 00	
for Deaf and Dumb, ...	24,457 07	
Indians, ...	3,186 14	
Pensions, ...	406 00	
State Paupers, ...	124,092 69	
Transportation, . . .	12,218 64	
School for Idiots, ...	22,314 58	
Eye and Ear Infirmary, ...	5,000 00	
Home for Friendless Women and Children, .	2,000 00	
House of the Angel Guardian, . . .	2,000 00	
Board of State Charities, ...	32,342 45	
Settlement and Bastardy Cases, . . .	1,955 55	
Washingtonian Home, ...	6,000 00	
Coroners' Accounts, ...	544 96	
New England Home for Women and Children,	1,000 00	
		430,279 84

Military.

Adjutant-General and Clerk, ...	$4,500 00	
Extra Clerks, . . .	16,360 00	
Carried forward, ...	$20,860 00	$1,251,879 40

Brought forward, ...	$20,860 00	$1,251,879 40
Adjutant-General Incidentals, ...	2,541 84	
Massachusetts Bounty Records, . . .	1,999 41	
Monthly Bounties, ...	403 99	
Instruction, Orderly, and Roll Books, . .	201 50	
Armory Rents, ...	26,071 67	
Quartermaster-General and Ordnance Department, ...	11,072 66	
Quartermaster Supplies, ...	125,195 59	
State Aid, Cities and Towns, ...	648,380 60	
Non-residents, ...	7,318 67	
Military Accounts, ...	35,399 79	
Bounty and Claim Agency, . . .	6,030 03	
Paymasters' Monthly Bounty, . . .	1,974 40	
Volunteer Bounty, ...	1,225 00	
Military Fund, ...	108 34	
Testimonials for Soldiers and Sailors, . .	30 00	
Militia Bounty, ...	121,828 25	
Employment Bureau for Soldiers, . . .	2,500 00	
Expenses Bounty Commissioners, . . .	33 10	
Soldiers' National Cemetery, . . .	69 25	
Military Elections, ...	10 00	
Medical Supplies, ...	281 90	
Discharged Soldiers' Home, ...	3,000 00	
Surgeon-General's Department, . . .	7,569 99	
Expense on account State Aid, . . .	286 53	
		1,024,392 51
Reformatory and Correctional.		
State Police, ...	$153,880 78	
Expenses State Prison, ...	104,083 11	
State Reform School for Boys, .	57,145 12	
Nautical Branch School for Boys, .	55,924 22	
Industrial School for Girls, .	28,537 10	
Asylum for Discharged Female Prisoners, .	2,500 00	
Arrest of Fugitives, ...	965 55	
Agent for Discharged Convicts, . .	1,992 21	
		405,028 09
Public Buildings.		
Bridgewater Almshouse, ...	$828 58	
Tewksbury "	5,103 08	
Monson "	1,832 48	
State Prison, ...	33,124 85	
Reform School for Boys, ...	1,541 66	
Nautical Branch Reform School, . .	2,457 20	
		44,887 85
Carried forward, ...		$2,726,187 85

Brought forward, ...		$2,726,187 85
State Library.		
Librarian and Clerks, ...	$3,428 34	
State Library, Books, &c., . . .	3,578 16	
		7,006 50
Miscellaneous.		
Worcester County, Free Institute of, &c., .	$50,000 00	
Liquor Commissioner, ...	870 97	
Corporation Tax, ...	1,050,720 05	
Alien Estates, ...	265 34	
Alien Passengers, ...	6,128 00	
Repairs of Alien Passengers' Office, . .	996 38	
Dividend Tax, ...	5 33	
Inspector of Gasmeters, ...	3,000 00	
Rhode Island Boundary, ...	83 40	
Emergency Fund, ...	3,232 16	
Agricultural College, ...	50,000 00	
Census Abstract, ...	156 00	
Weights, Measures, &c., ...	208 00	
Sheriffs' Accounts, ...	372 48	
Massachusetts Acts and Resolves, . .	300 00	
Reception of President of United States, . .	718 11	
State Board of Health, ...	352 23	
Williams College, ...	25,000 00	
Gratuities, ...	2,565 00	
Museum of Zoölogy, ...	25,000 00	
Annuities of Martha Johonnot, . .	1,280 00	
New Salem Academy, ...	5,000 00	
Commissioners on Harbors and Flats, . .	562 00	
on River Fisheries, . .	6,845 67	
Coast Defences, ...	27,071 08	
Harbor Commissioners, ...	10,222 77	
Bureau of Statistics of Labor, . . .	2,626 54	
Premium on Gold, ...	170,561 37	
War Loan Sinking Fund, ...	175,250 00	
Bounty Loan Sinking Fund, . . .	20,000 00	
National Bank Tax, ...	121 78	
Normal School Buildings, ...	4,004 50	
		1,643,519 16
Interest.		
Interest on Deposit Loan, ...	$109 08	
on Three Years' Loan, . . .	47,221 14	
on Revision Statute Loan, . .	7,500 00	
on Almshouse Loan 1852, . .	4,950 00	
on Almshouse Loan 1853, . .	3,000 00	
on Almshouse Loan 1854, . .	3,025 00	
Carried forward, ...	$65,805 22	$4,376,713 51

Brought forward, ...	$65,805 22	$4,376,713 51
Interest on State House 1853, ...	3,250 00	
on State House 1854, . . .	4,725 00	
on Lunatic Hospital and State Prison 1854, ...	4,675 00	
on Lunatic Hospital Northampton 1857,	3,270 00	
on Public Debt 1861, ...	9,515 00	
on Union Loan, ...	209,400 00	
on Coast Defence, ...	44,450 00	
on Bounty Fund Loan, . . .	464,500 75	
on Back Bay Lands Loan, . . .	10,937 50	
on War Loan, ...	210,735 00	
on Temporary Loan, ...	41,644 08	
to Massachusetts Volunteers, . .	573 69	
on Deposits, ...	32 72	
		1,073,513 96
		$5,450,227 47

PAYMENTS ON LOANS, SINKING FUNDS AND OTHER ACCOUNTS.

Norwich and Worcester R. R. Sinking Fund, .	$10,000 00	
Bonds and Mortgages Railroad Corporations, .	3,102,440 00	
Western Railroad Sterling Loan, . . .	435,600 00	
Eastern Railroad Loan.	75,000 00	
Western Railroad Loan Sinking Fund, . .	329,927 30	
Public Debt Loan, ...	2,000 00	
Sales Back Bay Lands, ...	458,767 67	
Back Bay Lands Commissioners, . . .	186,235 12	
Notes and Mortgages Back Bay Lands, . .	373,804 76	
Interest on Notes and Mortgages Back Bay Lands, ...	20,465 19	
Income School Fund, 1868, . . .	84,578 58	
" " " " . . .	392 51	
Income Todd Normal School Fund, . .	1,483 26	
School Fund for Indians, . . .	78 00	
Rogers Book Fund, . . .	120 00	
W. & F. Shanly Conditional Certificates, .	340,000 00	
Deposit Loan, ...	6,125 80	
Temporary Loan, ...	1,114,102 95	
Three Years Loan, ...	916,124 25	
Baring Brothers & Co., ...	107,101 62	
Transactions with the Funds, . . .	2,017,725 76	
South Boston Flats, ...	545,505 00	
Income Agricultural Fund, ...	13,553 28	
Norwich and Worcester Railroad, . . .	24,000 00	
Eastern Railroad, ...	11,875 00	
Carried forward, ...	$10,177,006 05	$5,450,227 47

Brought forward, ...	$10,177,006 05	$5,450,227 47
Income Back Bay Lands Fund, . . .	6,600 67	
Troy and Greenfield R. R. and Hoosac Tunnel,	91,448 34	
Interest on Loan to Troy and Greenfield Railroad and Hoosac Tunnel, ...	261,176 11	
Massachusetts Volunteers, ...	2,712 83	
Paymasters' Suspense Account, . . .	1,474 46	
Recruitment Fund, ...	200 00	
Paymasters' Recruitment Fund, . . .	1,894 10	

Educational Expenses.

Secretary Board of Education,	. $3,400 00		
Printing for " "	10,948 23		
Members travelling Expenses,	. 191 90		
Agent of the Board, . .	. 3,183 33		
Incidentals of the Board, . .	. 39 75		
Support of Normal Schools, .	. 40,000 00		
Aid to pupils of Normal Schools,	. 4,000 00		
Teachers' Institutes, . .	. 3,000 00		
County Teachers' Association, .	. 225 00		
Massachusetts Teachers' Association,	800 00		
Indian Schools, . . .	. 599 00		
Normal School Buildings, .	. 11,245 50		
American Institute of Instruction,	. 500 00		
		78,132 71	
			10,620,645 27

Cash on hand,—

For account of Eastern Railroad Interest, .	$3,125 00	
of Norwich and Worcester Railroad Interest, ...	12,000 00	
of Almshouse Loan Sinking Fund,	5,147 47	
of Union Loan Sinking Fund, .	13 00	
of Bounty Loan Sinking Fund, .	174,026 04	
of War Loan Sinking Fund, .	166,374 56	
of Essex Bridge Fund, . . .	1,140 81	
of Harbor Compensation Fund, .	11,143 79	
of Coast Defence Loan Sinking Fund, ...	9,936 34	
of Troy and Greenfield Railroad Sinking Fund, ...	19,071 50	
of Recruitment Fund, . . .	1,149 46	
of Income Mass. School Fund, .	78,132 71	
of Income Todd Normal School Fund, ...	33 00	
of Income School Fund for Indians,	126 00	
of Income Rogers Book Fund, .	60 00	
Carried forward, ...	$481,479 68	$16,070,872 74

Brought forward, ...	$481,479 68	$16,070,872 74
For account of Commissioners Public Lands, .	56,928 68	
of Massachusetts Volunteers, .	49,439 84	
of Returned Allotments, . .	10 00	
of Allotment Rolls, . . .	284 34	
of Charles River and Warren Bridges Fund, ...	6,879 61	
of Income Agricultural Fund, .	2,588 00	
of Back Bay Lands Fund, . .	5,000 00	
of Boston, Hartford and Erie Railroad Sinking Fund, . . .	472,836 00	
of Temporary Loans, &c., . .	1,067,312 66	
		2,142,808 81
Total, ...		$18,213,681 55

TRANSACTIONS WITH THE FUNDS.

MASSACHUSETTS SCHOOL FUND.

Cash on hand January 1, 1869, . . .	$2,527 91	
Rec'd Town of Quincy, Note paid, . . .	10,000 00	
Eastern Railroad Bonds paid, . .	50,000 00	
Town of Provincetown Note paid, . .	500 00	
Town of Orono Bonds paid, . . .	5,000 00	
State of Maine Bonds paid, . . .	25,000 00	
J. White, Treas., unexpended moneys, .	718 10	
from Notes Back Bay Lands, . .	32,159 24	
unexpended moiety of Income, . .	9,012 44	
Town forfeitures, ...	4,782 31	
		$139,700 00

Payments for Investment.

For Note of Wilbraham, ...	$3,000 00	
Note of Quincy, ...	10,000 00	
Stock of Boston and Albany Railroad Company, ...	81,700 00	
Boarding-Houses Normal Schools, . .	45,000 00	
		139,700 00

Present Investments.

Note and Mortgage, ...	$15,000 00	
Board of Education, ...	45,000 00	
County, City and Town Notes and Bonds, .	387,153 32	
Notes and Mortgages Back Bay Lands undivided, ...	49,821 95	
United States 5-20 Bonds, . . .	30,000 00	
Massachusetts and other State Securities, .	761,000 00	
Western Railroad Stock 8,989 shares, .	915,428 50	
Total Fund, ...		2,203,403 77

CHARLES RIVER AND WARREN BRIDGES FUND.

Received for interest, ...	$4,706 30	
for rents, ...	2,101 77	
for sale of Malden note, . . .	17,500 00	
		24,308 07

Brought forward, ... $24,308 07

Payments.

For repairs, &c., ...	$15,438 06	
Discount on Malden note, ...	218 75	
Interest on advances from the Treasury, .	312 55	
Balance due Treasurer last year, . .	1,454 00	
		17,423 36

Cash on hand, January 1, 1870, . . . $6,884 71

Present Investments.

Massachusetts State Bonds, ...	$40,000 00	
City and Town Notes, Bonds, &c., . . .	19,000 00	
		59,000 00

Total Fund, ... $65,884 71

ALMSHOUSE LOAN SINKING FUND.

Cash on hand January 1, 1869, . . .	$4,757 29	
Received Interest on Fund, ...	7,963 68	
from Alien Passengers, . . .	6,000 00	
		18,720 97

Payments.

For Note of Town of Beverly, ...	$10,000 00	
Massachusetts War Loan and Interest, .	3,573 50	
		13,573 50

Cash January 1, 1870, ... $5,147 47

Present Investments.

Massachusetts State Scrip, ...	$104,611 00	
City and Town Notes and Bonds, . .	38,000 00	
		142,611 00

Total Fund, ... $147,758 47

BACK BAY LANDS SINKING FUND.

Received Eastern Railroad Loan paid in, . . . $25,000 00

Payments.

For Note Town of Billerica, ...	$10,000 00	
Note Town of Beverly, ...	10,000 00	
		20,000 00

Cash uninvested, ... $5,000 00

Brought forward, ... $5,000 00

Present Investments.

Massachusetts State Scrip, ...	$174,500 00	
Town Notes, ...	20,000 00	
Notes and Mortgages Back Bay Lands, . .	20,500 00	
		215,000 00

Total Fund, ... $220,000 00

ESSEX BRIDGE FUND.

Cash on hand January 1, 1869, . . .	$467 57	
Received for Sale of Old Material, . . .	300 00	
for Interest, ...	398 24	
		1,165 81

Payments.

Paid expenses, ... 25 00

Cash uninvested, ... $1,140 81

Present Investments.

Massachusetts State Bonds, ... 5,000 00

Total Fund, ... $6,140 81

WAR LOAN SINKING FUND.

Cash on hand, January 1, 1869, . . .	$4,526 39	
Received on Income War Fund, . . .	19,459 84	
on Income Union Fund since March 1, 1869, ...	124,264 70	
on Discount on Bonds purchased, .	3,600 00	
on Legislative Appropriation, . .	175,250 00	
on Sale of Land at Warren Bridge, .	5,825 72	
on Sale of Back Bay Land, . .	4,904 27	
on Interest on Back Bay Land Notes,	2,758 21	
on Sale of South Boston Flats to Boston, Hartford and Erie Railroad Company, . . .	545,505 00	
on Town of Randolph Note paid, .	5,000 00	
on Income Back Bay Land Sinking Fund, ...	9,813 17	
		$900,907 30

Payments.

For Note of Dukes County, . . .	$2,400 00	
Boston and Albany Railroad Stock, 606 shares, ...	60,627 74	

Carried forward, ... $63,027 74

Brought forward, ...	$63,027 74	$900,907 00
For Bonds of City of Taunton, . . .	45,000 00	
Town of Rochester Note, ...	6,000 00	
Bonds City of Chelsea, ...	75,000 00	
Note and Mortgage Boston, Hartford and Erie Railroad Company, . . .	545,505 00	
		734,532 74
Cash uninvested, ...		$166,874 56

Present Investments.

Western Railroad Stock in War Fund, . .	$60,627 74	
City and Town Notes and Bonds, . . .	403,400 00	
Note Boston, Hartford and Erie Railroad Company, with mortgage, ...	545,505 00	
		1,009,532 74
Total Fund, ...		$1,175,907 30

TROY AND GREENFIELD RAILROAD LOAN SINKING FUND.

Cash on hand, January 1, 1869, . . .	$4,940 09	
Received on Income of Fund, ...	44,588 69	
for Note paid State Treasurer, . . .	1,000 00	
for Note paid West Brookfield, . .	2,000 00	
for Discount on Malden Note, . .	218 75	
		$52,747 53

Payments.

For Notes of Town of Medway, . . .	$4,000 00	
Notes of Town of Dartmouth, . . .	6,000 00	
Massachusetts Bonds, War Loan, . .	4,000 00	
Accrued Interest, ...	470 13	
Engraving and Printing Scrip, . . .	1,705 90	
Note of Town of Malden, . . .	17,500 00	
		33,676 03
Cash uninvested, ...		$19,071 50

Investments.

City and Town Notes, Bonds, &c., . . .	$421,543 00	
United States Bonds, 6 per cent., . . .	27,500 00	
State Scrip, ...	150,500 00	
		599,543 00
Total Fund, ...		$618,614 50

COAST DEFENCE LOAN SINKING FUND.

Cash on hand, January 1, 1869, . . .	$6,849 18	
Received on Income of Fund, ...	23,087 16	
for Note paid Town of Westfield, .	5,000 00	
		$34,936 34

Brought forward, ...		$34,936 34

Payments.

For Notes of Rowley, ...	$5,000 00	
Notes of Town of Beverly, . . .	20,000 00	
		25,000 00

Cash uninvested, ...		$9,936 34

Present Investments.

State Scrip, ...	$115,000 00	
City and Town Notes and Bonds, &c., . .	274,000 00	
.		389,000 00

Total Fund, ...		$398,936 34

BOUNTY LOAN SINKING FUND.

Cash on hand, January 1, 1869, . . .	$16,663 48	
Received on Income of Fund, ...	195,635 43	
of United States, ...	55,604 96	
for Sales of Back Bay Land, . .	224,479 57	
for Sales of Guns in London, . .	7,540 40	
for Interest on Back Bay Land Notes,	11,504 84	
for Legislative Appropriation, . .	20,000 00	
for West Roxbury Note paid, . .	5,000 00	
for South Reading Note paid, . .	10,000 00	
		$546,428 68

Payments.

For Note of Town of Medway, . . .	$20,000 00	
Bonds of City of Taunton, . . .	20,500 00	
Notes of Town of Ashby, ...	8,000 00	
of Town of Peabody, . . .	12,000 00	
of Town of Webster, . . .	15,000 00	
of Town of Rockport, . . .	15,000 00	
of Town of Wakefield, . . .	10,000 00	
Bonds of Massachusetts War Loan, . .	10,000 00	
Boston and Albany Railroad Stock, . .	40,400 00	
Notes of Town of Rockport, . . .	30,000 00	
of Town of Truro, ...	2,500 00	
of Town of Freetown, . . .	5,000 00	
and Mortgages Back Bay Land, .	183,916 44	
Accrued interest, &c., ...	86 20	
		372,402 64

Cash uninvested, ...		$174,026 04

Brought forward, ... $174,026 04

Present Investments.

Massachusetts Scrip in Fund, ...	$245,000 00	
City and Town Scrip, ...	523,032 77	
Boston and Albany Railroad Stock, . .	469,526 25	
State Scrip other than Massachusetts, . .	349,000 00	
Notes and Mortgages Back Bay Land, . .	333,252 56	
	———————	1,919,811 58

     Total Fund, ... $2,093,837 62

BOSTON, HARTFORD AND ERIE RAILROAD SINKING FUND.

Rec'd from Company Sept. 16, Cash, . .	$134,745 60	
from Company Oct. 21, Cash, . .	50,529 60	
from Company Nov. 5, Bonds pledged, .	286,334 40	
from Interest Nov. 25, . . .	1,608 52	
from Sale of Bonds pledged, . . .	281,469 18	
from Interest on uninvested money, .	1,167 03	
from Company for money loaned, &c., .	291,166 07	
from Treasurer of Commonwealth, borrowed, ...	101,059 20	
	———————	$1,148,079 60

Payments,—

For Note of State Treasurer, ...	$101,059 20	
Bonds taken as security, ...	286,334 40	
Note of Company, temporary loan, . .	200,000 00	
Note of Town of Beverly, . . .	20,000 00	
Note of Town of Brookline, . . .	67,800 00	
	———————	675,193 60

     Cash uninvested, ... $472,886 00

Now invested,—

City and Town Scrip, ...   87,800 00

     Total Fund, ... $560,686 00

NOTES AND MORTGAGES FOR BACK BAY LANDS.

Balance on hand, January 1, 1869, . . . $256,628 00
Received during the year, ... 350,374 64
$607,002 64
Received in payment of Notes and Mortgages, . . . 23,430 12

Total Notes and Mortgages, Jan. 1, 1870, . . $583,572 52

SCHEDULE OF NOTES AND MORTGAGES.

James Eaton, 4 notes, due 1 and 2 years from
April 9, 1863, . . . $11,246 50
6 notes, due 1, 2 and 3 years
from September 11, 1866, . 5,460 00
16,706 50

N. C. Munson, 9 notes, due 1, 2 and 3 years
from September 11, 1866, . $12,852 00
3 notes, due 1, 2 and 3 years
from July 12, 1869, . . 3,727 50
16,579 50

William Chadbourn, 2 notes, due 3 years from Sept. 29, 1863, 3,641 60
G. O. Shattuck, 1 note, due 2 years from January 3, 1864, . 882 00
F. Evans, 2 notes, due 1 and 2 years from Sept.
29, 1863, ... $3,921 74
6 notes, due 1, 2 and 3 years
from November 26, 1866, . 20,097 45
24,019 19

C. Francis, 2 notes, due 2 years from February 10, 1863, . 6,162 75
E. J. Browne, 2 notes, due 2 years from February 10, 1863, . 5,610 80
H. C. Stevens, 1 note, due April 9, 1865, ... 2,481 70
C. K. Kirby, 1 note, due April 9, 1864, . . $2,672 60
1 note, due April 9, 1865, . . 2,672 60
9 notes, due 1, 2 and 3 years
from April 30, 1869, . . 10,412 64
15,757 84

Chas. W. Freeland, 12 notes, due 1, 2 and 3 years from Sept.
11, 1866, ... 14,112 00
Samuel H. Gookin, 4 notes, due 2 and 3 years, from May 19,
1864, ... 6,720 00
T. J. Lee, 6 notes, due 2 and 3 years from May 19, 1864, . 9,072 00

Carried forward, ... $121,745 88

Brought forward, ...		$121,745 88
Thomas Richardson, 3 notes, due 2 and 3 years from May 19, 1864, ...		4,536 00
E. W. Cutler, 15 notes, due 1, 2 and 3 years from October 16, 1865, ...		30,468 30
Jarvis Williams, 2 notes, due 2 and 3 years from Oct. 16, 1865,		5,577 60
E. D. Jordan, 20 notes, due 2 and 3 years, from October 26, 1865, . . .	$42,638 40	
21 notes, due 1, 2 and 3 years from November 26, 1866, .	32,155 20	
12 notes, due 1, 2 and 3 years from December 24, 1868, .	15,330 00	
3 notes, due 1, 2 and 3 years from April 10, 1869, . .	24,675 00	
3 notes, due 1, 2 and 3 years from April 30, 1869, . .	6,652 80	
		121,451 40
Dwight Foster, 6 notes, due 1, 2 and 3 years from October 16, 1865, ...		10,886 40
Peter T. Homer, 6 notes, due 2 and 3 years from October 8, 1867, . .	$6,414 24	
6 notes, due 1, 2 and 3 years from October 30, 1869, .	7,665 00	
		14,079 24
D. Goodnow, 2 notes, due 2 and 3 years from June 16, 1868, .		2,016 00
Newton Talbot, 6 notes, due 1, 2 and 3 years from July 12, 1869, ...		10,836 00
F. H. Moore, 3 notes, due 1, 2 and 3 years, from July 12, 1869,		3,528 00
S. G. Palmer, 3 notes, due 1, 2 and 3 years from July 12, 1869,		3,675 00
Nathan Morse, 3 notes, due 1, 2 and 3 years from July 12, 1869, ...		3,675 00
C. B. Botsford, 8 notes, due 2 and 3 years from July 12, 1869,		9,800 00
H. W. Suter and O. A. Bingham, 12 notes, due 1, 2 and 3 years from December 24, 1869, . . .		8,400 00
George Wheatland, Jr., 3 notes, due 1, 2 and 3 years from Dec. 24, 1868, .	$7,119 00	
3 notes, due 1, 2 and 3 years from April 10, 1869, . .	16,023 00	
3 notes, due 1, 2 and 3 years from April 30, 1869, . .	5,733 00	
		28,875 00
F. W. & C. B. Sawyer, 3 notes, due 1, 2 and 3 years from December 24, 1868, ...		4,462 50
A. B. Almon, 3 notes, due 1, 2 and 3 years from December 24, 1868, ...		5,040 00
Carried forward, ...		$359,052 32

Brought forward, ...		$359,052 32
G. M. Gibson, 3 notes, due 1, 2 and 3 years from December 24, 1868, ...		4,462 50
Leopold Morse, 3 notes, due 1, 2 and 3 years from December 24, 1868, ...		8,085 00
Old South Society, 4 notes, one on demand for,	$5,000 00	
3 notes, due 1, 2 and 3 years,		
from October 30, 1869, . .	30,000 00	
		35,000 00
Samuel Bigelow, 3 notes, due 1, 2 and 3 years, from April 10, 1869, ...		14,196 00
William Thomas, 3 notes, due 1, 2 and 3 years from April 30, 1869, ...		3,780 00
Jacobs & Deane, 12 notes, due 1, 2 and 3 years from April 10, 1869, ...		17,766 00
J. Lawrence and T. J. Coolidge, 30 notes, due 1, 2 and 3 years from April 30, 1869, ...		36,441 30
H. B. Richmond, 24 notes, due 1, 2 and 3 years from April 10, 1869, ...		41,790 00
Bezar Thayer, 3 notes, due 1, 2 and 3 years from October 30, 1869, ...		3,528 00
David Hunt, 3 notes, due 1, 2 and 3 years from October 30, 1869, ...		7,056 00
D. B. Flint, 3 notes, due 1, 2 and 3 years from October 30, 1869, ...		3,528 00
Chas. A. Wood, 12 notes, due 1, 2 and 3 years from October 30, 1869, ...		18,887 40
		$583,572 52

Belonging to the Following Funds.

Bounty Loan Sinking Fund, ...	$333,252 56	
Commissioners Public Lands, ...	179,998 00	
Massachusetts School Fund, ...	49,821 95	
Back Bay Lands Sinking Fund, . . .	20,500 00	
		$583,572 51

STATEMENT

Of sums remaining unpaid January 1st, 1870, on Warrants drawn in 1869, and the names of the parties to which said sums are due, as per Sect. 4th, Chapter 1st, of Acts of 1858.

No. of Roll.	No. of Warrant.	PERSON OR CORPORATION.	Amount.	Total.
		Coroners.		
11		Geo. Blatchford, ...	$0 58	
12		J. Moody, ...	58	
13		W. Smith, ...	5 00	
14		E. W. Rand, ...	2 74	
15		Wm. Kuhl, ...	2 74	
16		J. M. Tappan, ...	2 74	
17		C. L. Ayers, ...	2 74	
18		G. W. Brown, ...	2 74	
20		W. H. Fitts, ...	2 60	
21		T. W. Foster, ...	3 00	
22		C. A. Nolin, ...	58	
23		J. Dixon, ...	1 16	
24		F. L. Mason, ...	1 16	
25		A. A. Hoyt, ...	58	
26		D. Thayer, ...	2 00	
48		Wm. Kelley, ...	58	
49		R. Kelley, ...	58	
50		R. A. Hall, ...	58	
52		Asa Hall, ...	1 37	
53		K. K. Morrison, ...	1 37	
54		H. A. Akin, ...	1 37	
55		R. N. Holman, ...	1 37	
56		W. M. Ryan, ...	1 37	
57		J. Hopkins, ...	1 37	
58		E. Mason, ...	62	
59		M. Norton, ...	62	
60		T. Scannel, ...	62	
61		J. J. Moore, ...	62	
62		E. H. Smith, ...	62	
63		William Ryan, ...	2 04	
75		S. H. Todd, ...	58	
76		H. Steele, ...	58	
77		George B. Stevens, . . .	58	
79		R. Fisher, ...	58	
81		S. E. Stockwell, ...	58	
82		J. L. Eldridge, ...	58	
83		S. Flannagan, ...	58	
		Carried forward, . . .	$50 10	

STATEMENT—Continued.

No. of Roll.	No. of Warrant.	PERSON OR CORPORATION.	Amount.	Total.
		Brought forward, . . .	$50 10	
		Coroners—Continued.		
84		A. N. Norcross, ...	58	
85		J. Dunn, ...	58	
101		A. B. Brown, ...	1 78	
102		G. H. Chesley, ...	58	
103		J. A. Dole, Jr., ...	58	
19		J. M. Carter, ...	2 74	
113		F. Wheeler, ...	58	
114		E. K. Tibbetts, ...	58	
125		G. H. Hope, ...	66	
134		William Bush, ...	2 74	
135		G. Barber, ...	2 74	
136		J. Barney, ...	5 74	
137		E. Churchill, ...	2 74	
138		H. H. Cunnis, ...	58	
139		C. H. Fitch, ...	2 74	
140		P. Fitzgerald, ...	5 74	
141		J. W. Jordan, ...	2 74	
142		C. L. Prouty, ...	2 74	
143		F. H. Rice, ...	5 16	
144		H. L. Shumway, ...	1 50	
146		Albert Wood, ...	58	
148		H. M. Kimball, ...	2 00	
149		—— Soule, ...	50	
150		William West, ...	2 00	
180		T. Harris, ...	2 40	
181		E. B. Moore, ...	2 00	$103 40
		Military Accounts.		
909		J. C. Weller, ...	$10 00	
916		G. H. Knapp, ...	2 00	
919		S. Hayward, ...	12 00	
926		D. A. Donaldson, ...	2 00	
927		C. I. Bullard, ...	2 00	
928		J. G. Smith, ...	4 00	
929		R. F. Prentiss, ...	4 00	
930		M. P. Pierce, ...	5 40	
933		J. L. Kingman, ...	25 00	
948		R. L. B. Fox, ...	25 00	
955		J. B. Pendergast, ...	25 00	
956		J. M. Torrey, ...	25 00	
980		J. F. Searle, ...	25 00	
989		L. Cummings, ...	25 00	
992		H. M. McIntire, ...	25 00	
994		C. Roby, ...	25 00	
1,002		G. S. Merrill, ...	33 70	
1,058½		A. Cloutman, ...	3 50	
		Carried forward, . . .	$278 60	

STATEMENT—Continued.

No. of Roll.	No. of Warrant.	PERSON OR CORPORATION.	Amount.	Total.
		Brought forward, . . .	$278 60	$103 40
		Military Accounts—Continued.		
1,059½		M. E. Bigelow, ...	5 25	
1,060½		C. A. Davis, ...	3 50	
1,061½		H. Litchfield, ...	3 75	
1,062½		J. Stratman, ...	2 25	
1,063½		M. C. White, ...	5 25	
1,067		P. A. O'Connell, ...	1 75	
1,068		D. S. McNamara, ...	1 75	
1,069		J. M. Tobin, ...	1 75	
1,070		E. Flatherty, ...	1 75	
1,071		D. O. Sullivan, ...	1 75	
1,072		C. Shepard, ...	1 75	
1,081		D P. Vant, ...	4 00	
1,086		P. C. H. Belcher, ...	4 00	
1,087		J. W. McKenzie, ...	1 80	
1,098		A F. Stevens, ...	7 40	
1,107		G. W. Fuller, ...	5 40	
1,116		J. O'Neil, ...	1 75	
1,125		N. F. Appolonio, ...	5 00	
1,126		G. R. Alaxander, ...	1 75	
1,128		E. D. Chase, ...	1 75	
1,132		L. A. Cook, ...	1 40	
1,134		W. Graves, ...	1 75	
1,136		P. L. Lambert, ...	1 75	
1,137		C. Lambert, ...	1 75	
1,138		William W. Mann, . . .	1 75	
1,139		D. McDonald, . . .	1 75	
1,141		A. E. Proctor, ...	1 75	
1,143		R. Simpson, . . .	1 75	
1,144		G. M. Tufts, . . .	1 75	
1,145		J. D. White, ...	1 75	
1,150		S. E. Atwood, ...	12 28	
1,152		B. F. Butler, ...	13 80	
1,159		E. P. Bowen, ...	14 84	
1,165		S. P. Bowland, ...	3 00	
1,166		W. Burnham, ...	13 08	
1,170		G. J. Carney, ...	13 40	
1,171		C. Curtis, ...	3 24	
1,179		B. Doral, ...	14 84	
1,183		J. J. Eaton, ...	6 84	
1,188		S. Flagg, ...	14 52	
1,193		A. Geyer, ...	5 16	
1,195		Y. G. Hurd, ...	13 40	
1,197		C. W. Howland, ...	4 60	
1,201		E. Hunt, ...	12 44	
1,205		W. Ingals, ...	11 00	
1,207		E. J. Jones, ...	11 00	
		Carried forward, . . .	$526 54	

STATEMENT—Continued.

No. of Roll.	No. of Warrant.	PERSON OR CORPORATION.	Amount.	Total.
		Brought forward, . . .	$526 54	$103 40
		Military Accounts—Concluded.		
1,219		J. McArdel, ...	11 00	
1,225		T. F. Martin, ...	3 88	
1,234		William H. Page, . . .	11 00	
1,235		G. H. Pierson, . . .	12 60	
1,241		J. L. Robinson, . . .	12 76	
1,249		E. Sutton, ...	13 40	
1,251		N. Taylor, ...	14 84	
1,252		G. H. Thorn, . . .	3 00	
1,258		C. G. Usher, . . .	11 80	
1,259		C. W. Vaughn, . . .	5 80	
1,261		H. W. Wilson, . . .	11 16	
1,263		W. H. Whitney, . . .	3 00	
1,268		C. A. Wheeler, . . .	14 60	
1,706		A. Freeman, . . .	5 00	
1,707		N. T. Opolonio, . . .	5 00	
1,708		C. E. Spaulding, . . .	1 75	
1,709		G. C. Craig, . . .	1 75	
1,710		J. H. Cook, . . .	1 75	
1,711		G. S. Brown, . . .	1 75	
1,712		G. H. Drew, . . .	1 75	
1,713		A. P. Sanborn, . . .	1 75	
1,714		J. W. W. Marjoram, . . .	1 75	
1,715		T. P. Bowers, . . .	1 75	
1,716		T. E. Austin, . . .	1 75	
1,717		William Bra_bson, . .	1 75	
1,718		A. Poggie, . . .	1 75	
1,719		A. Gallagher, . .	1 75	
1,720		C. Messenger, . . .	1 75	
1,721		G. A. Meacham, . . .	12 60	
1,722		C. W. Slack, . . .	5 00	
1,129		G. P. Bancroft, . . .	1 75	
1,131		E. D. Chase, . . .	1 75	
	347	George S. Merrill, . .	4 26	
	571	J. B. Parsons, . . .	2 00	
	571	H. W. Abbott, . . .	3 20	
	571	E. A. Ramsey, . . .	1 20	
	700	Western Union Telegraph Co., .	1 94	
				721 83
		Militia Bounty.		
1,365		H. N. Nilson, ...	$7 50	
1,367		G. J. Arnold, ...	7 50	
1,371		Charles Curtis, . . .	2 00	
1,372		G. W. Sargent, . . .	7 50	
1,379		George L. Miller, . . .	2 00	
1,385		W. H. Page, . . .	7 50	
1,386		S. B. Bowland, . . .	2 00	
		Carried forward, . . .	$36 00	$825 23

STATEMENT—Continued.

No. of Roll.	No. of Warrant.	PERSON OR CORPORATION.	Amount.	Total.
		Brought forward, . . .	$36 00	$825 23
		Militia Bounty—Continued.		
1,387		G. H. Thorn, ...	2 00	
1,388		William H. Whitney, . . .	2 00	
1,394		J. L. Robinson, . . .	7 50	
1,395		J. R. Thurston, . . .	7 50	
1,396		E. Hunt, ...	7 50	
1,397		William N. Taylor, . . .	2 00	
1,399		T. F. Martin, ...	2 00	
1,450		H. W. Nilson, . . .	1 00	
1,461		H. M. Abbott, . . .	2 00	
1,462		T. J. Borden, . . .	1 90	
1,463		E. P. Clark, . . .	2 00	
1,464		E. D. Capron, . . .	2 00	
1,465		L. Day, ...	2 00	
1,466		B. D. Davol, . . .	1 90	
1,467		J. J. Eaton, ...	1 90	
1,468		D. B. N. Fish, . . .	2 00	
1,469		T. A. Francis, . . .	2 00	
1,470		C. H. Flanders, . . .	2 00	
1,471		H. G. Gilman, . . .	2 00	
1,472		J. R. Hunt, . . .	2 00	
1,473		E. S. Holcomb, . . .	2 00	
1,474		W. F. Harrington, . . .	2 00	
1,475		J. L. Knight, . . .	2 00	
1,476		J. B. Parsons, . . .	2 00	
1,477		George H. Knapp, . . .	2 00	
1,478		F. A. Rust, . . .	2 00	
1,479		S. B. Spooner, . . .	2 00	
1,480		S A. Sargent, . . .	2 00	
1,481		William H. Sisson, . . .	2 00	
1,483		N. Taylor, . . .	1 90	
1,484		O. Ward, ...	2 00	
1,486		Co. B, Third Regiment, . .	15 20	
1,489		E, Third Regiment, . .	26 00	
1,491		G, Third Regiment, . .	15 75	
1,493		I, Third Regiment, . .	18 00	
1,497		W. W. Burnham, . . .	50	
1,505		Co. C, Sixth Regiment, . .	10 00	
1,506		D, Sixth Regiment, . .	14 00	
1,507		E, Sixth Regiment, . .	36 00	
1,509		G, Sixth Regiment, . .	11 00	
1,510		H, Sixth Regiment, . .	8 00	
1,516		C. E. Spaulding, . . .	1 10	
1,517		G. H. Thorn, . . .	1 10	
1,518		Co. A, Seventh Regiment, . .	17 60	
1,520		D, Seventh Regiment, . .	13 20	
1,521		E, Seventh Regiment, . .	15 40	
		Carried forward, . . .	$315 95	

STATEMENT—Continued.

No. of Roll.	No. of Warrant.	PERSON OR CORPORATION.	Amount.	Total.
		Brought forward, . . .	$315 95	$825 23
		Militia Bounty—Concluded.		
1,522		Co. F, Seventh Regiment, . .	15 40	
1,525		B. F. Boynton, . . .	4 00	
1,526		J. F. Kimball, . . .	4 00	
1,529		B F. Peach, Jr., . . .	4 00	
1,552		Co. D. Tenth Regiment, . . .	32 00	
1,557		I, Tenth Regiment, . . .	13 20	
1,558		K, Tenth Regiment, . . .	24 00	
1,559		B. F. Butler, ...	88 00	
1,561		G. J. Carney, . . .	33 00	
1,562		Y. G. Hurd, ...	77 00	
1,563		E. J. Jones, ...	99 00	
1,565		E. J. Sherman, . . .	110 00	
1,566		R. G. Usher, ...	66 00	
1,579		C. Curtis, ...	15 00	
1,586		H. W. Wilson, . . .	55 00	
1,587		T. J. Borden, . . .	55 00	
1,589		E. P. Bowen, . . .	55 00	
1,591		B. D. Davol, . . .	55 00	
1,593		C. W. Holland, . . .	15 00	
1,594		N. Taylor, ...	55 00	
1,595		C. M. Vaughn, . . .	15 00	
1,602		W. H. Page, . . .	55 00	
1,604		G. H. Thorn, . . .	15 00	
1,605		W. H. Whitney, . . .	15 00	
1,612		J. McArdel, . . .	55 00	
1,615		W. A. McDonald, . . .	15 00	
1,636		G. H. Pierson, . . .	55 00	
1,637		E. Sutton, . . .	55 00	
1,638		E. S. Atwood, . . .	55 00	
1,646		W. R. Nichols, . . .	15 00	
1,650		A. H. Whidden, . . .	15 00	
1,652		W. Burnham, . . .	55 00	
1,661		G. A. Whitney, . . .	15 00	
1,664		A. Geyer, . . .	15 00	
1,667		E. Hunt, . . .	55 00	
1,671		J. L. Robinson, . . .	44 00	
1,673		W. H. Tozier, . . .	15 00	
1,677		S. Flagg, . . .	55 00	
1,696		J M. Drennan, . . .	55 00	
				1,864 55
		State Aid to Individuals.		
936		M. Chamberlain, . . .	$12 00	
968		E. S. Nutting, . . .	24 00	
1,000		E. Wilson, . . .	12 00	
1,006		E. L. Freeland, . . .	24 00	
1,707		C. Grennell, . . .	12 00	
		Carried forward, . . .	$84 00	$2,689 78

STATEMENT—Continued.

No. of Roll.	No. of Warrant.	PERSON OR CORPORATION.	Amount.	Total.
		Brought forward, . . .	$84 00	$2,689 78
		State Aid to Individuals—Con.		
1,021		J. B. Sheenan,	12 00	
51		S. A. Adams, .	12 00	
57		S. L. Bowen, .	24 00	
58		S. D. Blake, .	24 00	
69		J. Corkery, .	24 00	
70		M. W. Chamberlain,	12 00	
78		M. Eddy, .	24 00	
82		S. W. Gott, .	18 00	
87		E. L. Houghtting, .	24 00	
92		S. E. Lore, .	18 00	
94		L. C. Lakin, .	12 00	
96		A. L. McGee,	18 00	
103		A. L. Perkins,	24 00	
104		S. E. Porter, .	24 00	
108		M. A. Pearson,	24 00	
110		C. A. Rice, .	18 00	
111		M. H. Richards,	18 00	
115		S. A. Simmons,	24 00	
132		E. Wilson,	12 00	
133		J. Buckley, .	24 00	
134		D. Courser, .	24 00	
138		E. L. Freeland,	24 00	
139		C. Grinnell, .	12 00	
141		D. K. Hoffman,	12 00	
150		J. C. Sawyer,	12 00	
151		J. B. Sherman,	12 00	
155		H. E. Gilbert,	27 00	
157		S. A. Adams, .	12 00	
163		S. L. Brown, .	24 00	
164		S. D. Blake, .	24 00	
175		J. Corkery, .	24 00	
177		M. W. Chamberlain,	12 00	
184		M. Eddy, .	24 00	
188		S. W. Gott, .	18 00	
193		E. L. Houghtting, .	24 00	
198		S. C. Lore, .	18 00	
200		L. C. Lakin, .	12 00	
202		A. L. McGee,	18 00	
209		A. L. Perkins,	24 00	
210		S. E. Porter, .	24 00	
214		M. A. Pearson,	24 00	
216		C. A. Rice, .	18 00	
217		M. A. Richards,	18 00	
221		S. A. Simmons,	24 00	
238		E. Wilson,	12 00	
239		J. Buckley, .	24 00	
		Carried forward, . . .	$995 00	

STATEMENT—Continued.

No. of Roll.	No. of Warrant.	PERSON OR CORPORATION.	Amount.	Total.
		Brought forward, . . .	$995 00	$2,689 78
		State Aid to Individuals—Con.		
240		D. Courser, ...	24 00	
244		E. L. Freeland, . . .	24 00	
245		C. Grennell, ...	12 00	
247		D. K. Hoffman, . . .	12 00	
255		C. R. Parkhurst, . . .	24 00	
256		J. C. Sawyer, . . .	12 00	
257		J. B. Sherman, . . .	12 00	
268		S. A. Adams, ...	12 00	
274		S. L. Brown, . . .	24 00	
275		S. D. Blake, . . .	24 00	
276		E. Chapman, ...	24 00	
288		M. W. Chamberlain, . .	12 00	
289		J. Corcery, ...	24 00	
295		C. S. Day, ...	24 00	
296		M. Eddy, ...	24 00	
300		S. W. Gott, ...	18 00	
305		E. R. Houghtting, . .	24 00	
310		S. C. Lore, ...	18 00	
312		L. C. Lakin, . . .	12 00	
314		A. L. McGee, . . .	18 00	
320		J. E. C. Pratt, . . .	18 00	
321		A. L. Perkins, . . .	24 00	
322		S. E. Porter, . . .	24 00	
325		M. E. Parsons, . . .	18 00	
326		M. A. Pearson, . . .	24 00	
328		C. A. Rice, . . .	18 00	
329		M. H. Richards, . . .	18 00	
330		A. A. Snow, . . .	24 00	
333		S. A. Simmons, . . .	24 00	
350		E. Wilson, ...	12 00	
351		J. Buckley, . . .	24 00	
352		D. Courser, . . .	24 00	
353		T. Campbell, . . .	24 00	
356		E. L. Freeland, . . .	24 00	
357		C. Grennell, . . .	12 00	
359		D. K. Hoffman, . . .	12 00	
364		P. McMann, . . .	24 00	
367		C. R. Parkhurst, . . .	24 00	
369		J. L. Sherman, . . .	12 00	$1,737 00
		Witness Fees before Committees.		
1		W. Allen, ...	$0 72	
2		B. W. Bump, . . .	72	
4		J. Cole, Jr., . . .	72	
5		D. Cobb, ...	80	
6		—— Cobb, ...	80	
		Carried forward, . . .	$3 86	$4,426 78

STATEMENT—Continued.

No. of Roll.	No. of Warrant.	PERSON OR CORPORATION.	Amount.	Total.
		Brought forward, . . .	$3 86	$4,426 78
		Witness Fees—Continued.		
7		E. Dunham, ...	80	
8		E. W. Drake, ...	72	
9		J. M. Eddy, ...	80	
10		A. F. Finney, ...	72	
11		A. Pratt, ...	72	
12		Z. Pratt, ...	72	
13		W. L. Pierce, ...	72	
14		P. E. Pennyman, ...	72	
15		—— Pratt, ...	72	
16		D. Lucas, ...	72	
17		T Smith, ...	78	
18		G. L. Soule, ...	72	
19		A. O. Standish, ...	78	
20		E. C. Shaw, ...	80	
21		E. A. Shaw, ...	80	
22		S. Tucker, ...	72	
23		L. S. Thomas, ...	78	
24		C. B. Wood, ...	1 44	
25		J. T. Wood, ...	72	
26		J. F. Wood, ...	78	
27		J. Wood, ...	78	
28		E. R. Waters, ...	78	
29		C. C. Allen, ...	1 25	
30		N. Adams, ...	1 25	
33		E. B. Badger, ...	1 25	
34		C. Barney, ...	1 25	
37		A. Boyden, ...	1 25	
39		J. W. Bacon, ...	1 25	
41		S. W. Bates, ...	1 25	
43		F. Child, ...	2 50	
44		L. Child, ...	1 25	
45		C. Colier, ...	1 45	
47		C. Carpenter, ...	1 25	
49		J. A. Cunningham, . . .	1 25	
50		G. W. Chapman, ...	1 25	
51		S. Chapen, ...	11 30	
54		M. Crowley, ...	1 45	
55		M. Copey, ...	1 45	
57		H. G. Darrell, ...	2 05	
58		J. M. Dolliver, ...	1 25	
59		J. A. Dupee, ...	1 25	
60		T. Drew, ...	2 05	
61		M. E. Dow, ...	1 45	
62		G. E. Daily, ...	1 45	
63		J. B. Edmonds, ...	1 45	
64		C. Emerson, ...	3 75	
		Carried forward, . . .	$67 70	

STATEMENT—Continued.

No. of Roll.	No. of Warrant.	PERSON OR CORPORATION.	Amount.	Total.
		Brought forward, . . .	$67 70	$4,426 78
		*Witness Fees—*Continued.		
65		J. S. Eldridge, ...	2 50	
66		H. Flood, ...	3 75	
67		N. Freeman, ...	1 25	
68		J. Fedderhen, ...	1 25	
69		J. Fedderhen, 3d, . . .	1 25	
70		J Fitch, ...	1 25	
71		E D Foster, ...	2 50	
72		T. W. Fisher, ...	1 45	
73		S. Gore, ...	1 25	
74		G. Gibson, ...	1 45	
75		T. Gaffield, ...	1 25	
76		T. Gaffield, ...	3 75	
77		J. Green, ...	2 70	
78		J. A. Grant, ...	1 45	
79		S. G. Howe, ...	1 25	
80		W. O. Haskel, ...	3 75	
82		N. Harris, ...	1 25	
83		C. D. Head, ...	1 25	
84		H. P. Hanson, ...	1 25	
85		W. E. Hough, ...	1 25	
86		L Hutchins, ...	1 25	
87		S. Hall, Jr., ...	1 25	
88		I. A. Holmes, ...	4 05	
90		G. Hardy, ...	1 33	
92		H. Jewell, ...	1 25	
93		A. E. Johonnot, ...	1 25	
97		J. Kennelly, ...	1 25	
99		Ed. Kerr, ...	1 33	
102		W. B. Long, ...	1 45	
104		J. Louden, ...	1 25	
105		J. C. Loring, ...	2 50	
106		G. H. Marden, ...	2 50	
107		J. Mack, ...	1 45	
109		J. W. May, ...	1 25	
110		G. H. Morse, ...	2 50	
111		Wm. Mooney, ...	2 50	
112		D. Murphy, ...	1 45	
113		P. Milan, ...	3 30	
114		A. Mason, ...	1 33	
116		Wm. Nichols, ...	2 50	
117		N. C. Nash, ...	1 25	
118		R. C. Nichols, ...	2 50	
120		D. Page, ...	1 45	
122		R. K. Potter, ...	1 25	
123		C. Porter, ...	1 25	
124		J. F. Porter, ...	1 25	
		Carried forward, . . .	$150 64	

STATEMENT—Continued.

No. of Roll.	No. of Warrant.	PERSON OR CORPORATION.	Amount.	Total.
		Brought forward, . . .	$150 64	$4,426 78
		Witness Fees—Concluded.		
125		H. E. Pond, ...	2 50	
126		J. Parks, ...	5 20	
127		T. Parks, ...	1 45	
128		R. Payn, ...	3 75	
131		C. C. Richardson, . . .	1 33	
134		J. Shaughnessey, . . .	1 25	
135		R. Simpson, . . .	1 45	
136		F. Smith, . . .	2 50	
137		E. R. Smythe, . . .	1 25	
139		T. Sculley, . . .	1 45	
140		R. B. Shaw, . . .	2 58	
144		S. J. Tuttle, . . .	1 25	
145		J. W. Twombly, . . .	3 75	
146		J. E. Tyler, . . .	2 74	
147		William Washburn, . . .	25 00	
148		D. Washburn, . . .	1 45	
150		T. J. Whidden, . . .	2 50	
151		O. White, . . .	1 25	
152		G. W. Walker, . . .	1 25	
155		J. Woods, . . .	3 75	
156		C. T. Woodman, . . .	1 25	
157		J. C. Westcott, . . .	4 45	
158		J. S. Whitney, . . .	1 25	
160		W. Wyman, . . .	2 70	
161		L. L. White, . . .	1 45	
162		Dr. Walker, . . .	2 58	
163		G. W. Young, . . .	1 25	
94		C. Joy, ...	3 75	
				236 87
		State Police.		
245		N. C. Stearns, . . .	$6 65	
1,064		Boston Gas Light Company, . .	98.	
1,527		Boston Gas Light Company, . .	33	
137		Childs, Crosby & Lane, . .	41 66	
878		J. B. Frost, . . .	107 15	
726		J. B. Frost, . . .	151 60	
1,080		S. J. Fletcher, . . .	107 00	
1,195		H. Brigham, . . .	25 00	
1,211		E. Howard & Co., . . .	33 00	
1,412		T. Aldrich, . . .	87 00	
1,447		J. B. Frost, . . .	94 75	
1,557		J. B. Frost, . . .	97 05	
1,565		Beals, Greene & Co., . .	11 50	
1,574		Thayer & Dunham, . .	4 50	
				768 17
		Carried forward, . . .	. .	$5,431 82

STATEMENT—Continued.

No. of Roll.	No. of Warrant.	PERSON OR CORPORATION.	Amount.	Total.
		Brought forward, . . .	. .	$5,431 82
		District-Attorneys.		
1,400		E. J. Sherman, ...	$125 00	
1,108		W. W. Rice, ...	125 00	
1,404		E. B. Gillett, ...	125 00	
1,405		S. T. Spaulding, . . .	83 33	
1,083		W. W. Rice, ...	125 00	
1,034		E. B. Gillett, ...	125 00	
1,036		S. T. Spaulding, . . .	83 33	
		A. A. Abbott, ...	20 16	
				811 82
		Judges Superior Court.		
948		Otis P. Lord, ...	$350 00	
1,317		Otis P. Lord, ...	350 00	
1,318		E. Wilkinson, ...	350 00	
				1,050 00
		Judges Probate and Insolvency.		
957		Henry Chapin, ...	$208 33	
960		S. F. Lyman, ...	75 00	
1,327		W. A. Richardson, . . .	208 33	
1,328		Henry Chapin, ...	208 33	
1,329		S. F. Lyman, ...	75 00	
1,336		J. M. Day, ...	75 00	
				849 99
		Judges Police Courts.		
992		W. E. Currier, ...	$83 33	
994		J. Davis, ...	133 33	
1,001		J. Bacon, ...	66 66	
1,002		J. C. Ives, ...	41 66	
1,003		J. R. Bulkley, ...	25 00	
1,026		H. Williams, ...	166 66	
1,363		J Davis, ...	133 33	
1,361		W. E. Currier, ...	83 33	
1,371		J. Bacon, ...	66 67	
1,372		J. C. Ives, ...	41 67	
1,373		J. R. Bulkley, ...	25 00	
1,376		H. Williams, ...	166 67	
				1,033 31
		Clerks Police Courts.		
1,009		F. L. Porter, ...	$66 66	
1,010		A. B. Leonard, ...	66 66	
1,025		J. P. Ellis, ...	66 66	
1,379		F. L. Porter, ...	66 67	
1,380		A. B. Leonard, ...	66 67	
1,395		J. P. Ellis, ...	66 67	
				399 99
		County Teachers' Associations.		
	782	Barnstable County, . . .	. .	25 00
		Carried forward, . . .	. .	$9,601 93

CPSIA information can be obtained
at www.ICGtesting.com
Printed in the USA
BVHW041105111218
535332BV00008B/124/P